# *The Theology of Blood*

## *A Study in Scarlet*

King's Table Meeting
Memphis, Tennessee
September 28-30, 2016

**K.W. Bow**

Copyright 2016 by Kenneth W. Bow
The book author retains sole copyright to his contributions to this book.
Published 2016.
Printed in the United States of America.

All rights reserved.

No portion of this book may be reproduced, stored in a retrieval system, or transmitted in any form or by any means – electronic, mechanical, photocopy, recording, scanning, or other – except for brief quotations in critical reviews or articles, without the prior written permission of the author.

ISBN 978-1-9860028-8-5

Front cover design by Mark Gauthier.


This book was published by BookCrafters,
Parker, Colorado.
bookcrafterscolorado@gmail.com

This book may be ordered from
www.bookcrafters.net and other online bookstores.

# *Foreword*

I treasure the friendship and ministry of Doctor Kenneth Bow as one of God's most precious gifts to me.

For Forty years God has used him to bless His Kingdom and feed His people with the finest of the wheat.

Like Joshua the High Priest, he is among those men wondered at.

(Zech 3:8 Hear now, O Joshua the high priest, thou, and thy fellows that sit before thee: for they are men wondered at:)

Pastor Bow is revered by his generation, as a hero of the faith, a champion of truth, and preacher most beloved.

Not only is he my favorite preacher, but my hero as well. His ministry is without equal and as a writer he has no peer.

God has graced him with great understanding, wisdom, and anointing. Reading his books makes one feel as if they were reading the writings of the Apostle Paul. His Solomon-like wisdom shines through with amazing insight on every scripture.

You will love everything this man writes. Read and be blessed!

Martyn Ballestero

# Table of Contents

- Introduction: God's Sovereign Choice......................1
- The Blueprint: The Creation of Man........................3
- Healing..................................................................6
- Salvation..............................................................10
- The Voice of Blood...............................................14
- The Signet of the Covenant..................................19
- The Blood of Jesus Christ.....................................28
- The Seal of the Everlasting Covenant....................31
- Conclusion............................................................35
- Bibliography.........................................................37

# *Introduction*
# *God's Sovereign Choice*

Theology is the study of God. It extends to the study of religion. In the King's Table meeting it includes a distinctive body of theological opinion. A comprehensive study of the theology of blood would require many volumes. This dissertation will cover some of the major and salient points.

God is sovereign. God needs no reason nor justification for His choices. By His sovereign choice, blood is designed, and chosen, to perform certain functions. These functions are not necessarily connected or interlinked. The multi-purposes of blood in scripture is the choice of a sovereign God for His own purposes.

The sovereignty of God can be defined by the exercise of His own choice, for His own pleasure. God is infinitely elevated above the highest creation. God is subject to none, influenced by none, and is absolutely independent in His choices. The psalmist said, "whatsoever the Lord pleased, that did He in heaven, and in earth, in the seas, and all deep places."[1]

---

[1] Psalm 135.6 KJV Whatsoever the LORD pleased, that did he in heaven, and in earth, in the seas, and all deep places.

Blood is the choice of a sovereign God to propitiate healing, forgiveness, and cleansing to fallen man. A sovereign God chose blood to stand for surety of His divine covenants. The scriptures reveal that God chose the blood of animals under the first covenant to provide necessary provision for fallen mankind to be justified. Ultimately, this sovereign God would robe Himself in humanity, and shed His own blood, for the sin of all mankind. From His blood would come eternal forgiveness, sonship, and the surety of an unfailing new covenant. By His own blood would this sovereign God purchase the church.

We have no privilege to ask this sovereign God why He chose blood for these many purposes in His eternal plan. However, we may explore the theology of blood that He has chosen to reveal to us in Holy Writ.

# *The Blueprint:*
# *The Creation of Man*

Man was not the first of God's created entities to possess blood. Prior to man's creation, other living forms were created with blood as a necessary part of their existence. The function of blood can be observed and studied in many forms of the animal kingdom. For this treatise I choose to use the function of blood in man to illustrate God's blueprint for blood in relation to theology.

Blood is a body fluid in animals and man that delivers necessary ingredients to our cells and then removes metabolic waste from our circulatory system. Life giving elements like oxygen are supplied to our cells by blood. After our body has used the components we need, then blood takes the metabolic waste away for cleansing.

The blood brings a supply of nutrients such as glucose, amino acids, and fatty acids. This supply insures new life and provides immunological functions. The circulation of white blood cells allows our immune system to detect foreign material and send antibodies to provide healing and protection. When there is injury the blood coagulates and broken blood vessels begin to provide a semi-gel to stop bleeding. The blood is a messenger system that transports hormones when tissue is damaged. The blood regulates the body temperature.[2]

This metaphor is apropos. In our spiritual man, it is the blood of Jesus Christ that brings sonship and new birth. It is the same blood that jettisons our sins and failures to keep us in a state of acceptance and approval with God. New life is formed by the blood of Jesus Christ, then the blood of Jesus Christ removes the penalty of sin.

The cycle of constant blood flow also represents the purpose of the blood of Jesus Christ to mankind. The sentence of death placed upon man after the fall in Eden is irrevocable to mortal man. Mortal man will die. God did not revoke his sentence against fallen man. By divine infusion of His own blood, God provides man a solution to mortal death. Mortal death still comes to all of mankind. The answer to this mortal conundrum of death, is the continual flow of the blood of Jesus Christ. This is why Jesus proclaimed[3] "and whosoever liveth and believeth in me shall never die." The ERV version says "And everyone who lives and believes in me will never really die." It is this revelation of the blood of Jesus Christ that prompts the Apostle Paul to write "O death where is thy sting."[4] The death sentence against fallen man has been abrogated.

The blueprint is new life, and removal of harmful, life threatening entities. It is the constant flow of blood, both in natural man, and in spiritual man, that provides life. It is blood that defends, enables, purifies, rebuilds, and gives continual life. This is a small part of what we can know about a sovereign God who chose this marvelous

---

2 "Blood," Wikipedia
3 John 11.26 And whosoever liveth and believeth in me shall never ie.
4 1 Cor 15.55 KJV O death, where is thy sting? O grave, where is thy victory?

creation called blood, to fulfill His grand plan to redeem fallen humanity. Blood is our blueprint for everlasting life, and for the defeat of eternal death.

Blood is mentioned in the Bible hundreds of times. Moses, David, Peter, John and many others, all speak about the blood. There are terms used like precious, incorruptible, and overcoming to describe the blood. Lev 17.11 KJV says *the life of the flesh is in the blood.* This holds true in the physical realm and also in the spiritual realm. If for any reason the blood supply is cut off from any part of your body, that part of your body begins to die. This holds true in the spiritual sense as well. If we withhold the blood from flowing into areas of our life, that part of our life will spiritually die. This is potentially why people become immune in their conscience to guilt over repeated sin in their life. Eventually the conscience is severed, or dies. The sin is committed without remorse, and therefore it continues.

# *Healing*

*But unto you that fear my name shall the Sun of righteousness arise with healing in his wings; and ye shall go forth, and grow up as calves of the stall.*
*Malachi 4.2 KJV*

The sovereign God has granted healing (Heb: *Marpe*) to mankind. *Marpe* includes the idea of cure, curative, and deliverance as well as healing. Healing is also connected to the blood of Jesus Christ. While on earth for His earthly ministry, Jesus healed many. This power was also delegated to the disciples,[5] and later to the church through the gifts of the Spirit.[6]

Healing is a provision to us by a sovereign God. It is humanly provided in two ways. One is incorporated in the constant flow of blood that brings white blood cells that fight off sickness. When we would be sick, the blood fights it off, and we are never even aware our physical body has been invaded. The blood simply fought it off as a routine manner of created purpose.

The second way blood is used to provide healing in

---
[5] Matt 10.1 And when he had called unto him his twelve disciples, he gave them power against unclean spirits, to cast them out, and to heal all manner of sickness and all manner of disease.
[6] 1 Cor 12.9 To another faith by the same Spirit; to another the gifts of healing by the same Spirit;

our physical body is through an act of healing from science, or from God. This may occur through prayer. It can happen through corporate prayer when other believers join you in prayer. It can happen when you follow the admonition in James to call for the elders of the church, and they lay hands on you and pray.[7] It is of note that when a person is healed by the blood while being prayed for, their sins are also forgiven.[8] The word here is *hamartia*. It means abstract sins. This possibly means sins we are not aware of. The healing blood also removes the waste of sin that we are unaware of. It appears the blood of Jesus Christ potentially heals and forgives simultaneously. This poses a question: can the blood be applied to heal without activating forgiveness? Conversely, can the blood be applied to forgive and not heal?

The answer may lie in the blood itself. We know there are people healed by the natural process of the white blood cells, while at the same time not fending off another attack of sickness or disease. A person's immune system may repel a flu virus and yet accommodate certain diseases. In the spiritual realm, this may hold true also. While healing a sickness or disease the blood may not forgive known sins that are not repented of. If the sin has been repented of, the natural process of the blood removes the sin as waste material in our spiritual man. Sin that has not been repented of can abscess, or become abnormal growth. This is illustrated by sin repented of, and forgiven, in the act of repentance, but not removed until baptism.

---

7 James 5.14 Is any sick among you? let him call for the elders of the church; and let them pray over him, anointing him with oil in the name of the Lord:

8 James 5.15 And the prayer of faith shall save the sick, and the Lord shall raise him up; and if he have committed sins, they shall be forgiven him

Baptism becomes essential, not to remove sin, but rather to remove the sins that are forgiven. Peter spoke "be baptized every one of you for the remission of sins."[9] Remission is *aphesis* in the original language, and means freedom, pardon, or deliverance. This is the blood of Jesus Christ removing harmful wastes and past sins from our spiritual life. This is the purpose of the washing in baptism. Saul of Tarsus was instructed by Ananias to arise and be baptized and wash away thy sins.[10]

Throughout the Bible there is a recurring insight that God only sees the blood when the blood is applied. This was evident at the Passover. God did not see the failures and past sins of the Hebrew people. He saw the blood. When God saw the blood, judgment was averted. As they were required to apply the blood on their houses, and door posts, so we are required to apply the blood to our lives. This application of blood occurs when we confess our sins and ask forgiveness. If we confess our sins (*hamartia*), He is faithful to forgive our sins (*hamartia*),[11] and to cleanse us from all unrighteousness. The Greek word *pistos*, for faithful, means trustworthy.

Isaiah 53.5[12] says with his stripes we are healed. The Hebrew word here is raphah, which means to mend, to cure, or to heal. When Jesus died on Calvary he

---

9 Acts 2.38 Then Peter said unto them, Repent, and be baptized every one of you in the name of Jesus Christ for the remission of sins, and ye shall receive the gift of the Holy Ghost.
10 Acts 22.16 And now why tarriest thou? arise, and be baptized, and wash away thy sins, calling on the name of the Lord.
11 1 John 1.9 f we confess our sins, he is faithful and just to forgive us our sins, and to cleanse us from all unrighteousness.
12 Isaiah 53.5 But he was wounded for our transgressions, he was bruised for our iniquities: the chastisement of our peace was upon him; and with his stripes we are healed.

purchased our salvation. Heb 9.22[13] informs us that without shedding of blood, there is no remission (pardon) of sins. While Jesus was shedding His blood for the sins of the world, He was also providing healing through that same blood. To deny the blood provides healing denies a primary purpose of the blood of Jesus Christ.

---

13 Heb 9.22 And almost all things are by the law purged with blood; and without shedding of blood is no remission.

# *The Name~Salvation*

*Then Peter said, Silver and gold have I none; but such as I have give I thee: In the name of Jesus Christ of Nazareth rise up and walk, Acts 3.6*

There is an undeniable connection between the name of Jesus and healing. Numerous times healing occurred by invoking the name of Jesus. Because of the connection between healing and salvation, the name is also imperative in salvation. Acts 4.12[14] states neither is there salvation in any other, for there is none other name under heaven whereby we must be saved. This shows the indivisible property of blood. When the blood is applied, it heals and it saves. In Acts chapter 3 the name of Jesus heals the lame man and in Acts chapter 4 the name is required for salvation.

It is at the moment of salvation that the blood provides forgiveness and cleansing. The blood cannot be applied except through the name of Jesus. Forgiveness requires blood to be shed. Sins must be covered, and blood is the entity God has chosen to cover sin. This concept had its genesis in Genesis. Cain's sacrifice was not accepted while Abel's sacrifice was pleasing to God. It was the

---

14 Acts 4.12 Neither is there salvation in any other: for there is none other name under heaven given among men, whereby we must be saved.

sacrifice that included the shedding of blood that was acceptable to God. This template of the blood of an animal covering sin in the opening chapters of the Bible, would prove to be the method of forgiveness for the next four thousand years. This would be consummated and fulfilled in the shedding of blood on Calvary by Jesus Christ, who is the Lamb of God slain from the foundation of the world.[15]

The importance of the name is demonstrated in the book of Acts which is the history of the New Testament Church. One the first day of the church in Acts 2,[16] the admonition was to repent and be baptized in the name of Jesus Christ. When salvation went to the Samaritan people in Acts 8,[17] the name is again pre-imminent. When the gospel is preached for the first time in an environment of gentile people in Acts 10,[18] again the name is paramount to salvation. In Acts 19,[19] when Paul encounters disciples of John the Baptist, the name of Jesus is center stage. This ratifies Acts 4.12 that neither is there salvation in any other name. The name of Jesus must be used in salvation. Jesus is the one who shed his blood on the cross. God's requirement for forgiveness and cleansing is blood. This leads to the name of Jesus invoking the blood when it is spoken. This happens

---

15 Rev 13.8 And all that dwell upon the earth shall worship him, whose names are not written in the book of life of the Lamb slain from the foundation of the world.
16 Acts 2.38 Then Peter said unto them, Repent, and be baptized every one of you in the name of Jesus Christ for the remission of sins, and ye shall receive the gift of the Holy Ghost.
17 Acts 8.12 But when they believed Philip preaching the things concerning the kingdom of God, and the name of Jesus Christ, they were baptized, both men and women
18 Acts 10.43 To him give all the prophets witness, that through his name whosoever believeth in him shall receive remission of sins.
19 Acts 19.5 When they heard this, they were baptized in the name of the Lord Jesus.

at baptism when the name of Jesus is invoked, and it also happens at prayer for healing.

The blood of Jesus applied at salvation is permanent. It cannot be removed. The blueprint is in our natural blood again. Many times when a crime is committed the criminal attempts to wash away the blood so he can remove evidence. Bleach can remove a bloodstain to the naked eye, but forensic experts can use the application of luminol to show that hemoglobin is present. Even if the criminal washes the the bloodstained item of clothing 10 times, the light from luminol still reveals blood.[20] Luminol is a substance that emits a blue glow when mixed with the right oxidants. Forensic experts use luminol at crime scenes to detect traces of blood.

The spiritual analogy is true as well. There is no element that can remove the blood of Jesus once it has been applied to a life. When the light of God shines on a life, the glow of the blood shows up and nothing can remove the blood once it has been applied.

When you exercise a muscle to the point of fatigue often you feel a burning in the muscle. This is caused by the buildup of lactic acid in the muscle. Lactic acid is a by-product of normal muscle contraction, and when it accumulates it can be mildly toxic to the muscle. Much like sin in our spiritual man. Fortunately, when lactic acid builds up during intense contractions, it is quickly swept away by the bloodstream and transported to the liver where it can be changed and used for fuel. Without this constant cleansing of the muscles even simple muscle movements would be nearly impossible because of pain. The blood is constantly exchanging the lactic acid for nutrients that the muscles can use for

---

20 "Detecting Evidence After Bleaching;" exploreforensics.co.uk

further activity. This principle of exchange is seen in everything the blood does for the body. This also is true in the spirit.

It is especially seen in the provision of salvation. It is this constant flow of grace and mercy to our lives that keeps us saved. People who lack this understanding often fear the coming of the Lord. They fear there will be some unknown sin that will keep them out of heaven. This concept of continual blood flow is the simple answer to the guilt and defeat Satan tries to inject into the minds of believers. The blood works even when you do not feel it, or when you are not aware. The blueprint of the human body shows us that the blood never stops working in us and for us. This is one reason why the doctrine of predestination can be understood. To stay in the church, which is predestinated, means we stay in a place of constant blood flow and cleansing. There is no need to fear the coming of Jesus Christ, for when he appears we will be clean and pure. We will be purged of all dead works.[21] The constant flow of the blood of Jesus will have removed any dead works.

---

21 Heb 9.14 How much more shall the blood of Christ, who through the eternal Spirit offered himself without spot to God, purge your conscience from dead works to serve the living God

# *The Voice of Blood*

*Genesis 4.10 the voice of thy brother's blood crieth unto me from the ground.*

Blood has a voice. God heard the voice of Abel's blood crying out from the ground. It was innocent blood. In searching out the blueprint of the blood in the genus of man, one thing becomes clear and consistent throughout all the Old Testament. Innocent blood has a voice that cries out to God.

Many times in the Bible God commanded people to shed blood. At times God himself shed blood. Sometimes it was thousands and even tens of thousands of people. It seemed to please God and He directed it at times. The shed blood of the guilty, silenced the voice of judgment.

When innocent blood was shed, it was entirely different. It required a payment in blood. *So ye shall not pollute the land wherein ye are: for blood it defileth the land: and the land cannot be cleansed of the blood that is shed therein, but by the blood of him that shed it.*[22] Defile here means to soil in a moral sense. It required blood to remove the stain and penalty of innocent blood. This eternal

---

[22] Numbers 35.33 So ye shall not pollute the land wherein ye are: for blood it defileth the land: and the land cannot be cleansed of the blood that is shed therein, but by the blood of him that shed it.

truth of innocent blood is continuous throughout the Old Covenant. In Deut 19.10 it states *That innocent blood be not shed in thy land, which the LORD thy God giveth thee for an inheritance, and so blood be upon thee.*[23] When time had passed, and it seemed murder had gone unavenged, God remembered. In 1 Kings 2.31 David instructs Benaiah to fall upon Joab and kill him for the innocent blood Joab had shed.[24] One of the indictments against the wicked King Manasseh was that he shed innocent blood very much, till he had filled Jerusalem[25] The nation of Israel was indicted by God for their shedding of innocent blood.[26] According to Proverbs God hates seven things, and one of those seven things is hands that shed innocent blood.[27] The nation of Israel had a promise to dwell in the land if they did not shed innocent blood.[28] The nations of Egypt and Edom both were made a desolation because they shed innocent blood.[29]

## What is it about innocent blood that brings this strong

[23] Deut 19.10 That innocent blood be not shed in thy land, which the LORD thy God giveth thee for an inheritance, and so blood be upon thee.
[24] 1 Kings 2.31 And the king said unto him, Do as he hath said, and fall upon him, and bury him; that thou mayest take away the innocent blood, which Joab shed, from me, and from the house of my father.
[25] 2 Kings 21.16 Moreover Manasseh shed innocent blood very much, till he had filled Jerusalem from one end to another; beside his sin wherewith he made Judah to sin, in doing that which was evil in the sight of the LORD.
[26] Psalm 106.38 And shed innocent blood, even the blood of their sons and of their daughters, whom they sacrificed unto the idols of Canaan: and the land was polluted with blood.
[27] Prov 6.17  A proud look, a lying tongue, and hands that shed innocent blood,
[28] Jer 7.6-7. If ye oppress not the stranger, the fatherless, and the widow, and shed not innocent blood in this place, neither walk after other gods to your hurt: Then will I cause you to dwell in this place, in the land that I gave to your fathers, for ever and ever.
[29] Joel 3.19 Egypt shall be a desolation, and Edom shall be a desolate wilderness, for the violence against the children of Judah, because they have shed innocent blood in their land.

judgement from God? It was innocent blood in Egypt, painted on the doorpost, that repelled judgment and death. In the blueprint of God's plan, the voice of blood overcomes the voice of guilt and condemnation. At the Passover Jesus celebrated with His disciples, He clearly stated the cup was His blood of the New Testament which was shed for many for the remission of sins. It was the blood of Jesus that purchased the Church of God.[30] All of these instances show that innocent blood has a voice that God hears. It was not the shedding of blood that evoked a strong response from God, but rather the shedding of innocent blood. Israel was instructed to not avenge the blood of a thief who was guilty.[31]

The most telling verse about the voice of blood is found in Heb 12.24.[32] Jesus' blood speaks better things than that of Abel. If the blood of Abel speaks to God, how much better (stronger), does the voice of Jesus speak loud and clear. When a believer is born again, the blood of Jesus Christ is applied to their life. This application of blood constantly declares we are innocent. When the blood is applied, God only sees the blood. Satan and our flesh want to make us feel guilty and unworthy and condemned. If we could hear the supernatural voices from another world, we would hear the voice of the blood of Jesus proclaiming us innocent.

According to Rabbi Yonason Denebeim,[33] the voice of innocent blood has to do with the improbable marriage of the spirit and the body. This creates a soul. This voice

---

30 Acts 20.28 Take heed therefore unto yourselves, and to all the flock, over the which the Holy Ghost hath made you overseers, to feed the church of God, which he hath purchased with his own blood.
31 Ex 22.2 If a thief be found breaking up, and be smitten that he die, there shall no blood be shed for him.
32 Heb 12.24 And to Jesus the mediator of the new covenant, and to the blood of sprinkling, that speaketh better things than that of Abel.
33 Rabbi Yonason Denebeim, rabbi@chabadps.com

of innocent blood, according to Rabbi Denebeim, is the voice of the soul. When asked why the guilty do not have this voice, his answer was because the body was in control when sin was committed, and not the soul. The Rabbinical position is the soul cannot truly express itself through the medium of the flesh and bone, or words and language. These means of expression are inadequate to express the spiritual concepts and understandings. This explanation states all of us have thoughts and feelings we are incapable of articulating. These thoughts are recognizable but not ever spoken. The Rabbis believe this is the voice of our soul. Their position is our soul has no adequate way to speak. God alone can, and does, hear the cry of the soul in the case of innocent blood.

This Rabbinical concept does not align with numerous verses that equate innocent blood with someone who has not sinned. It also does not explain why the sin of the guilty is silent before God. The thief who is caught in the act does not have innocent blood. His thoughts had to have been involved and included intent, and prior thinking. This is illogical and unbiblical thinking on innocent blood.

When Judas Iscariot betrayed the innocent blood of Jesus,[34] there is no indication he operated totally by his flesh and did not use his mental faculties. Surely this decision was made not just in his physical body, but in his heart, the seat of affection and desire. The Rabbinical position is untenable and unsupported.

The innocent blood of the Old Covenant represents the coming blood of Jesus Christ. Jesus Christ is the final innocent blood. When Judas betrayed Jesus he betrayed

---

34 Matt 27.4 Saying, I have sinned in that I have betrayed the innocent blood. And they said, What is that to us? see thou to that.

"the innocent blood." Innocent blood has a voice. It has had a voice since the first murder in the Bible. Innocent blood is heard by the Sovereign God. Today the innocent blood of Jesus has a voice that proclaims freedom from judgment and penalty. When the blood of Jesus Christ has been applied to a life, there is a voice silently saying innocent. To an ear able to hear in the nether world, every believer walking through this world, would hear the repeated exclamation, innocent, innocent. The blood of Jesus Christ speaks louder and stronger than the blood of Abel.

## *The Signet of the Covenant*

*Exodus 24.8 And Moses took the blood, and sprinkled it on the people, and said, Behold the blood of the covenant, which the LORD hath made with you concerning all these words.*

A covenant with the sovereign God requires blood. God chose blood as the seal and the sign of this covenant. A covenant is a treaty, or a contract between two parties. Lesser covenants all had signs. The rainbow was the sign of the covenant with Noah. Circumcision was the sign of the covenant between God and Abraham. At times the covenant was described by way of metonymy. In Acts 7.8[35] the covenant with Abraham is described as "the covenant of circumcision." The relationship between the sign and the thing signified is important in the language of covenants. When Jesus instituted the Lord's supper, as they were eating the bread, He said, "this is my body."[36] He then gave them the cup and said "For this is my blood of the New Testament."[37] These

---

35 Acts 7.8 And he gave him the covenant of circumcision: and so Abraham begat Isaac, and circumcised him the eighth day;
36 Matt 26.26 And as they were eating, Jesus took bread, and blessed it, and brake it, and gave it to the disciples, and said, Take, eat; this is my body
37 Matt 26.28 For this is my blood of the new testament, which is shed for many for the remission of sins.

were the signs of the new covenant, the body and blood of Jesus Christ.

The new covenant had been foretold by Jeremiah when the teenage boy prophet prophesied in Jer 31.31[38] This was the covenant Jesus was establishing at the Passover supper. This covenant was also sealed with blood, the blood of Jesus Christ. This covenant established by the death of Jesus Christ is known as the everlasting covenant.[39]

Paul Ziegler writes on the website systemath.com[40]

*In ancient times the blood covenant was common among almost all of the people of the middle east. It was a way of establishing a binding contract between two men. What we call the Old and New Testaments could easily be called the Old and New Covenants. The typical blood covenant contained nine parts, or steps. These steps are as follows,*

*1) The two people exchange coats or robes. To a Hebrew, the coat or robe represented the person himself; even his very life itself.*

*2) They take off their belt and offer it to the other person. The belt, also called the girdle, was used to hold your sword, your knife, and other fighting instruments. In this way you were saying to the other person that you were offering him your protection. If someone attacks you, they also have me to deal with. Your battles are my battles.*

*3) Cut the covenant. In this part, an animal is killed and*

---

38 Jer 31.31 Behold, the days come, saith the LORD, that I will make a new covenant with the house of Israel, and with the house of Judah:
39 Heb 13.20 Now the God of peace, that brought again from the dead our Lord Jesus, that great shepherd of the sheep, through the blood of the everlasting covenant,
40 The Blood Covenant, Paul Ziegler, systemath.com

*cut down the middle and the two halves are laid opposite each other. The two parties to the covenant pass between the two halves of the animal and are saying, "May God do so to me and more if I break this covenant. This is a blood covenant, and can not be broken."*

*4) Raise the right arm and cut the palm of the hand and clasp each other's hand and mingle your blood. This is saying to the other person, "We are becoming one with each other." To intermingle the blood is to intermingle the very life of both people.*

*5) Exchange names. Each one takes part of the other's name and incorporates it into their own.*

*6) Make a scar or some identifying mark. The scar was the outward evidence of the covenant that others could see and know that the covenant was made. Sometimes they would rub the cut in the hand to make the scar, then anyone who wanted to fight you would know that he not only had to fight you but another as well.*

*7) Give terms of the covenant. Both parties to the covenant stand before a witness and list all of their assets and liabilities, because each one takes all of these upon himself. You are saying, "Everything I have is yours and everything you have is mine." If something happens to you, your covenant partner will see to it that your wife and children are taken care of.*

*8) Eat the memorial meal. A loaf of bread is broken in half. Each feeds his half to the other saying, "This is my body, and I am now giving it to you." Then they take wine as a symbol of his blood and say, "This is my blood which is now your blood."*

*9) Plant a memorial tree.. The two then plant a tree as a*

*memorial to the covenant and sprinkle it with the blood of an animal that was killed for the covenant offering.*

*These nine steps do not have to take place in the same order that they are listed here. There are a lot of covenants listed in the Bible and there is not great detail about them because everyone was familiar with the procedure and the writer assumes that we know what was done.*

*In our Bible we have the old and new testament, (or covenant). The old covenant was made with Abram and we have a record of it in the Bible. We can look in on it starting in the fifteenth chapter of Genesis. In verse one we read:* **"After these things the word of the Lord came to Abram in a vision, saying, 'Do not fear, Abram, I am a shield to you; Your reward shall be very great.'"** *Here we see God offering His robe and belt to Abram. He offers to be his shield and His rewards. He cuts the covenant in Genesis 15:7-21* **"And He said to him, 'I am the Lord who brought you out of Ur of the Caldeans, to give you this land to possess it.' So He said to him, 'Bring Me a three year old heifer, and a three year old male goat, and a three year old ram, and a turtle dove, and a young pigeon.' Then he brought all these to Him and cut them in two, and laid each half opposite the other; but he did not cut the birds. And the birds of prey came down upon the carcasses, and Abram drove them away. Now when the sun was going down, a deep sleep fell upon Abram; and behold, terror and great darkness fell upon him. "And God said to Abram, 'Know for certain that your descendants will be strangers in a land that is not theirs, where they will be enslaved and oppressed four hundred years. But I will also judge the nation whom they will serve; and afterward they will come out with many possessions. And as for you, you shall** *go to your fathers in peace; you shall be buried at a good old age. Then in the fourth generation they call return here, for the iniquity of the Amorite is not yet complete.' And it came about when the sun had set, that it was very dark, and behold, there appeared a smoking oven and a flaming torch which passed between these pieces. On that day, the Lord made a covenant with Abram, saying, 'To your descendants I have given this land, from the river of Egypt as far as the great river, the river Euphrates; the Kenite and the Kenizzite and the Kadmonite and the Hittite and the Perizzite and the Rephaim and the Amorite and the Canaanite and the Girgashite and the Jebusite.'." Here, God is giving the terms of the covenant to Abram. But who are the ones passing between the pieces while Abram is in the deep sleep? I submit to you that it is.... Christ. In the Revelation 1:14-15 we see a description of Christ as follows,* **"And His head and His hair were white like wool, like snow, and His eyes were like a flame of fire; and His feet were like burnished bronze, when it has been caused to glow in a furnace, and His voice was like the sound of many waters,"** *Here we see Christ, a descendant of Abram, standing in for Abram in the covenant procession. In Genesis 17:4-5,15 we see the exchange of names as follows,* **"As for Me, behold, My covenant is with you, and you shall be the father of a multitude of nations. No longer shall your name be called Abram, but your name shall be Abraham; for I will make you the father of a multitude of nations.... Then God said to Abraham, as for Sarai your wife, you shall not call her name Sarai, but Sarah shall be her name."** *In Hebrew, God was call YHWH. Here we see Him taking part of His name and combining it with that of Abram and Sarai. From that time on God was known as, "The God of Abraham." Next we see the making of a scar or* *symbol of the covenant. In Genesis 17:10-12 we see,* **"This is My covenant, which you shall keep, between Me and you and your descendants after you; every male among you who is eight days old shall be circumcised throughout your generations, a servant who is born in the house or who is bought with money from any foreigner, who is not of your descendants."** *The scar of circumcision bears witness of the covenant. Abraham was tested when God told him to sacrifice his only son Isaac on a mountain called mount Moriah near the town of Salem. Abraham passed the test. Two thousand years ago, the other party to the covenant was to sacrifice His only Son. The names had been changed by then; Salem was Jerusalem and Moriah had been changed to Calvary, but the places were the same.*

*The new covenant took place in the same area of the world and contained some of the same players. God was there, of course, and Jesus; now incarnate, and the descendants of Abraham. This time Jesus was not only the representative of Abrahams descendants but He was also the offering; the Lamb that was slain. This time it was God's only Son and not Abraham's. Let us see how the new covenant was completed in Christ.*

*1) Exchange the coats or robes. We come to this covenant clothed in sin and unrighteousness. We put on His righteousness. II Corinthians 5:21,* **"He made Him who knew no sin to be sin on our behalf, that we might become the righteousness of God in Him."** *He takes our sins upon Him and we take His holiness for ours. What an exchange!*

*2) Take off belt. He protects us and provides us with protection. Luke 10:19,* **Behold, I have given you authority to tread upon serpents and scorpions, and over all the** *power of the enemy, and nothing shall injure you."* Ephesians 6:13-17 *"Therefore take up the full armor of God, that you may be able to resist in the evil day, and having done everything, to stand firm. Stand firm therefore, having girded your loins with truth, and having put on the breastplate of righteousness, and having shod your feet with the preparation of the gospel of peace; in addition to all, take up the shield of faith with which you will be able to extinguish all the flaming missiles of the evil one. And take the helmet of salvation, and the sword of the Spirit, which is the word of God."*

3) Cut the covenant. Hebrews 10:14-18, *"For by one offering He has perfected for all time those who are sanctified. And the Holy Spirit also bears witness to us; for after saying, 'This is the covenant that I will make with them after those days, says the Lord: I will put my laws upon their heart, and upon their mind I will write them, And their sins and their lawless deeds I will remember no more. Now where there is forgiveness for these things, there is no longer any offering for sin,"* Jesus was not only the one making the covenant, but he was also the sacrificial lamb.

4) Raise right and and mix blood. Jesus was both man and God. He was holy and also human. As we have the shed blood of Jesus Christ applied to our hearts, His blood cleanses us from all sin and we are also made holy. Our lives are forever intermingled with His.

5) Exchange names. Jesus took on the name, "Son of Man" and we take on the name Christian. We are forever in the family of God.

6) Make a scar. Jesus has the scars of the nails in His

*hands and the feet and the scar of the spear in His side. We have the circumcision of the heart. Romans 2:29,* **"But he is a Jew who is one inwardly; and circumcision is that which is of the heart, by the Spirit, not by the letter; and his praise is not from men, but from God."*

*7) Give the covenant terms. Jesus gives the terms of the covenant in the whole Bible. It is our responsibility to know it so that we can live by it.*

*8) Eat memorial meal. I Corinthians 11: 23-26,* **"For I received from the Lord that which I also delivered to you, that the Lord Jesus in the night in which he was betrayed took bread; and when He had given thanks, He broke it, and said, 'This is my body, which is for you; do this in remembrance of Me.' For as often as you eat this bread and drink the cup, you proclaim the Lord's death until He comes."**

*9) Plant a memorial tree. The cross that Jesus died on was the tree that the blood of the sacrifice was sprinkled on and it is still a memorial of his covenant with us to this day.*

There are many variations of this blood covenant in Hebrew history. The primary point is the blood. No covenant was sealed until blood was involved. This is why Jesus is the mediator of the New Covenant as well as the high priest. He is the lamb of the New Covenant, for He is the one who shed His blood.

There are minor covenants in the Old Testament. Examples of these would be the Noahic, the Abrahamic, and the Davidic. The big picture is there are two covenants. There is the Old and the New. In the Old Testament, minor covenants are under the canopy of the larger covenant of blood sacrifice of animals. Covenant is also translated testament. Both the Old and the New Covenant were sealed by blood. The old was sealed with the blood of an animal, the new with the blood of Jesus Christ. Without the blood, the covenant was of none effect. This is the choice of a sovereign God.

## *The Blood of Jesus Christ*

*Forasmuch as ye know that ye were not redeemed with corruptible things, as silver and gold, from your vain conversation received by tradition from your fathers; But with the precious blood of Christ, as of a lamb without blemish and without spot: 1 Peter 1.18-19*

Never in the history of planet earth has there been blood like the blood of Jesus Christ. Never since the death of Jesus Christ has there been blood like the blood of Jesus Christ. His blood stands alone in its power and purpose. A sovereign God created this magnificent element for His own purposeful pleasure.

This blood came from the seminal line of Adam and the seminal line of God Himself when the Holy Ghost overshadowed the Virgin Mary.[41] Jesus Christ was God manifest in the flesh. This symbiotic element is like no other in the history of creation.

Peter called this blood precious (valuable, costly, honored, esteemed). It is this blood that redeems man from his fallen condition. Jesus Christ bare our sins

---

[41] Matt 1.18 Now the birth of Jesus Christ was on this wise: When as his mother Mary was espoused to Joseph, before they came together, she was found with child of the Holy Ghost.

upon the tree of Calvary. He drank the cup of our sins in the garden of Gethsemane. Somehow the ingestion of our sins into his body produced a vaccine for sin. He who knew no sin, took sin into himself, and His blood overcame the sin of the world.

Jesus is the expiator of our sins.[42] This blood is so powerful it is the propitiation for every person who ever calls on the name of Jesus. All future and past generations are saved by this blood if they call on the name of Jesus and obey the gospel.

This fact alone separates His blood from all others in world history, past, present, or future. It was the shedding of this blood of Jesus Christ that sealed the New Covenant. This had been planned from the foundation of the world. The crucifixion did not catch God unaware. It was God's everlasting plan. Jesus was the lamb slain from the foundation of the world.[43]

On a hot April afternoon outside the city of Jerusalem, a Roman soldier plunged a spear into the side of Jesus Christ while Jesus hung on the cross. Out of that wound flowed much more than blood and water. Out of that wound flowed the seal of the new covenant, the everlasting covenant, and the purchase of the church.[44] That blood, that day over two millennia ago, has forgiven millions of fallen humanity and is as powerful today as it was the day it flowed for the first time. Jesus Christ was the Lamb of God.

---

42 1 Jn 2.2 And he is the propitiation for our sins: and not for ours only, but also for the sins of the whole world.
43 Rev 13.8. And all that dwell upon the earth shall worship him, whose names are not written in the book of life of the Lamb slain from the foundation of the world.
44 Acts 20.28 Take heed therefore unto yourselves, and to all the flock, over the which the Holy Ghost hath made you overseers, to feed the church of God, which he hath purchased with his own blood.

To compute the volume of blood that has been shed since the dawn of time is unfathomable. First there is the blood of mankind shed in innumerable wars and killings. Thousands and thousands of lives in local wars, regional wars and world wars, has produced a virtual river of blood. To that we must add the thousands and thousands of animals offered for sacrifice throughout man's duration on earth. This river of blood can never be measured. We do know it was not enough. Sacrifices continued to be offered. Until the moment Jesus offered his blood on the cross, heaven was still saying it was not enough. At that moment, for the first time in heaven's history, it was recorded, "It is finished."[45] It was enough. Sacrifice was ended. As the lamb of God, Jesus, entered into the holiest of all and sat down, for the work of sacrifice was over. There has never been blood like Jesus' blood. It is unique in all of history. It was the blood of God himself, flowing through the literal body God created for himself. That marvelous blood now flows through every believer who obeys the gospel of Jesus Christ.

---

45 Jn 19.30 When Jesus therefore had received the vinegar, he said, It is finished: and he bowed his head, and gave up the ghost.

# *The Seal of the Everlasting Covenant*

*And he causeth all, both small and great, rich and poor, free and bond, to receive a mark in their right hand, or in their foreheads: And that no man might buy or sell, save he that had the mark, or the name of the beast, or the number of his name.*
*Revelation 13.16-17.*

This passage certainly ranks as one of the foremost Bible passages in today's world. Prophecy advocates hang their entire scope of prophetical fulfillment on this one passage. There is much discussion about the mark or seal that will be used by this future beast. Volumes have been written about who the candidate is, what the mark itself will be, and how it will be implemented.

Interestingly, the servants of God are also sealed with a mark. This mark identifies true believers on the earth during the same time as the mark of the beast. It seems odd that not much is written about this mark on God's servants as it is just as definite as the other mark upon the unfaithful.

*And I saw another angel ascending from the east, having the seal of the living God: and he cried with a loud voice to the four angels, to whom it was given to hurt the earth and the*

*sea,Saying, Hurt not the earth, neither the sea, nor the trees, till we have sealed the servants of our God in their foreheads.*
*Revelation 7.2-3*

How is blood related to this mark upon God's people? We know God seals His people because of passages like 2 Cor 1.22.[46] In that verse the word seal means to stamp with a signet of private mark. Paul uses the same Greek word (sphragizo) again in Eph 1.13,[47] where we are sealed after we believed. We are sealed with the holy Spirit of promise. Paul uses sphragizo to further state in Eph 4.30[48] we are sealed unto the day of redemption. This is the same word used in Rev 7.3[49] where the angel cries to hurt not the trees until we have sealed (sphragizo) the servants of our God in their foreheads. The servants of God have a stamp or private mark in their forehead, as well as the followers of the beast have their mark of 666 in their forehead.

Heb 13.20[50] is clear that the blood is the seal of the everlasting covenant of God. Believers are sealed with the holy Spirit of promise, sealed until the day of redemption, and sealed by God to protect them during the time period recorded in Revelations. While the followers of the beast have a mark in their forehead to show their allegiance, the children of God have a mark in their forehead to show their salvation and preservation.

---

46 2 Cor 1.22 Who hath also sealed us, and given the earnest of the Spirit in our hearts.
47 Eph 1.13 In whom ye also trusted, after that ye heard the word of truth, the gospel of your salvation: in whom also after that ye believed, ye were sealed with that holy Spirit of promise,
48 Eph 4.30 And grieve not the holy Spirit of God, whereby ye are sealed unto the day of redemption.
49 Rev 7.3 Saying, Hurt not the earth, neither the sea, nor the trees, till we have sealed the servants of our God in their foreheads.
50 Heb 13.20 Now the God of peace, that brought again from the dead our Lord Jesus, that great shepherd of the sheep, through the blood of the everlasting covenant,

What was true in the Old Covenant is true in the New Covenant. Atonement, rescue, redemption, and salvation is by the life, the blood of Christ. It was not his death in totality that provided all these things, but rather the blood that came from that death. In the case of a leper, his only hope was for someone to give him their blood.[51] This gift meant the giver must die to donate his blood so the leper could be cleansed. It was not the death of the donator, but the blood he gave that saved the life of the leper. When we partake of the divine nature,[52] we share the blood of God himself.[53] As the Father had life, so he gave to the son also to have life in himself. The life is in the blood.[54] The process was life for life, not death for life. It was Christ's life, his blood that gives us life, that is the seal of the everlasting covenant. The covenant is in life, eternal life, and not in death. It is no longer an altar of sacrifice where we meet God in a rite of death. It is now a table of communion where we meet him, and celebrate life and that more abundantly.

This supreme sacrifice by Jesus Christ was made once and for all. To question the sufficiency of His blood is to count the blood of the covenant an unholy or common thing. This would do despite unto the Spirit of grace.[55]

---

51 The Blood Covenant, Trumbull, pg 287
52 2 Pet 1.4 Whereby are given unto us exceeding great and precious promises: that by these ye might be partakers of the divine nature, having escaped the corruption that is in the world through lust.
53 Jn 5.26 For as the Father hath life in himself; so hath he given to the Son to have life in himself;
54 Lev 17.11 For the life of the flesh is in the blood: and I have given it to you upon the altar to make an atonement for your souls: for it is the blood that maketh an atonement for the soul.
55 Heb 10.29 Of how much sorer punishment, suppose ye, shall he be thought worthy, who hath trodden under foot the Son of God, and hath counted the blood of the covenant, wherewith he was sanctified, an unholy thing, and hath done despite unto the Spirit of grace?

Now the God of peace, that brought again from the dead our Lord Jesus, that great shepherd of the sheep, through the blood of the everlasting covenant, Make you perfect in every good work to do his will, working in you that which is wellpleasing in his sight, through Jesus Christ; to whom be glory for ever and ever. Amen. Heb 13.20-21

The everlasting covenant was introduced and sealed with the blood of Jesus Christ. Paul said the cup of blessing which we bless, is it not a communion of the blood of Christ? The bread which we break is it not a communion of the body of Christ?[56] The covenant of bread is temporary, the covenant of blood is permanent. The covenant of bread secures a truce, the covenant of blood secures an eternal union. The covenant of bread gives nourishment, the covenant of blood gives life. The covenant of bread is a pledge of hospitality, it brings a person into human relations with those who offer it. The covenant of blood is personal and individual and everlasting. The covenant of bread, his body, is the mediatorship of Christ and will one day be surrendered.[57] The covenant of blood is eternal and will never pass away. The covenant of blood is life forevermore. The blood of Jesus Christ is the seal of the everlasting covenant.

---

[56] 1 Cor 10.16 The cup of blessing which we bless, is it not the communion of the blood of Christ? The bread which we break, is it not the communion of the body of Christ?
[57] 1 Cor 15.24 Then cometh the end, when he shall have delivered up the kingdom to God, even the Father; when he shall have put down all rule and all authority and power

# *Conclusion*

A sovereign God chose in his infinite wisdom how to eternally bond us to himself. His sovereign choice was the bond of life in the blood, and not in the bond of death, as in all other world religions. In this, Christianity stands alone among all the religions of man. All other religions point to death and the end of life. Christianity points to death and the beginning of life forevermore, and immortality.

The blueprint of this plan by a sovereign God is the creation of man, God's highest order of creation. In man we find the blueprint of how this relationship of blood works. The blood brings nourishment and removes toxic and deadly entities from the body. The blood is ever flowing and is the essence of life itself. To lose blood is to lose life. To give blood is to give life.

The blood of Jesus Christ brings healing. It replaces polluted blood with sickness and viruses with pure blood, and therefore gives life.

The blood of Jesus Christ brings salvation to lost humanity. Herein is the manifesto of Jesus Christ. Life is given to man who is under the sentence of death, due to the fall of Adam in Eden.

The blood of Jesus Christ has a voice stronger than the voice of the blood of Abel. Blood has a voice. The blood of Jesus Christ is ever loudly proclaiming our redemption, our justification, and our sonship to God.

The blood of Jesus Christ is the seal and signet of the New Covenant. Without the blood of Jesus Christ there is no life, and Christianity sinks to the level of man made religion and joins the throng of hopeless, helpless, humanity. With the blood of Jesus Christ on a life there is a mark of ownership placed there by God himself.

The blood of Jesus Christ is unique above all blood ever shed in history. In the vast river of blood shed in wars and sacrifice, it stands alone in its efficacy. Jesus' blood alone saves mankind and gives mankind life for all eternity.

It the distant past of eternity, the sovereign God determined to provide fallible man with an infallible method of living forever, and defeated the sentence of death. This was done by placing His own efficacious blood as a seal on the forehead of his redeemed. The blood of Jesus Christ is the seal of the everlasting covenant.

In the study of the theology of blood we find the immutable, eternal, final solution to all man's failures. In the study of the theology of blood we find a sovereign God reaching to his fallen creation, and providing the answer to the dilemma all world religions seek to answer.

In the eons of eternity, it will ever be, the life is in the blood.

# *Bibliography*

Bible, KJV, 1611 Edition.

"Blood," Wikipedia, http://www.wikipedia.org

"Detecting evidence after bleaching," http://www.exploreforensics.co.uk

Paul Ziegler, "*The Blood Covenant*," http://www.systemath.com

Rabbi Yonason Denebeim, http://www.rabbi@chabadps.com

Trumbull, H. Clay, *The Blood Covenant*, New York, Charles Scribner's Sons, 1885

www.ingramcontent.com/pod-product-compliance
Lightning Source LLC
Chambersburg PA
CBHW040326300426
44112CB00021B/2890